*Anyone can take snaps these days, it's so simple and easy. But just occasionally you look at one and think, I'm proud of that, it's a very good picture. And then you start to wonder, how can I make a really good picture every time?*

*Colin Garratt (shown left) is a photographer of international repute, and has written this book to help you to be proud of every photograph you take, whatever camera you are using. If you are also interested in the way your camera works, you will find the answers to your questions in the Ladybird book* How it works: The Camera.

*Acknowledgments*

The author and publishers wish to thank the following for permission to reproduce paintings: page 47 (top) – Courtauld Institute Galleries, London; pages 11, 32 (bottom), 44 and 45 (top) – by courtesy of the trustees, National Gallery, London; page 47 (bottom) – by permission of Mrs C Spiers and the Tate Gallery; pages 45 (bottom) and 46 – The Tate Gallery; page 32 (top) – Crown Copyright, Victoria and Albert Museum; page 31 – the Science Museum, London; and page 12 – the Uffizi Gallery, Florence.

The photographs on pages 7, 10 (top), 13 (top and bottom), 17 (top), 26, 27, 29, 35 (bottom), 36 (bottom) and 37 are by Monica Gladdle, and contributions were also made by K Abbott, J Coles, A Freestone, M Johnson and R Wells. Cover photograph by Tim Clark.

Thanks are also due to Agfa-Gevaert Ltd, Kodak Ltd and VEB Pentacon Dresden for their help in supplying photographs and diagrams.

© LADYBIRD BOOKS LTD MCMLXXX

# Taking Photographs

*Text and photographs by* COLIN GARRATT

Ladybird Books Loughborough

# Chapter 1

# Photography and your camera

Photography provides us with a marvellous way of
expressing our thoughts and feelings. The origin of the
word comes from the Greek 'photos' meaning light, and
'graphos' meaning writing – writing with light. This is
exactly what we do whenever we take a photograph.

The creativity of photography is both exciting and
stimulating. The pictures we take provide us with a
wonderful diary of our life – a permanent record of
events, moods and places which have inspired us.

Sadly, many people shirk learning the fundamentals of
photography, fearing them to be too technical – too
many knobs and dials on the camera. Furthermore,
when it comes to making pictures they say, "Yes, I'd
love to, but I just don't have the eye for it."

The intention of this book is to allay such fears and
show that worthwhile pictures can be made with even the
simplest and cheapest cameras, once we have learnt to
recognise some of the magical ingredients which combine
to make good photographs.

But first let us consider the principal characteristics of
the simple camera as shown by picture *a*. The camera is
a light-tight box and the film, as shown in picture *b*, is
contained in an easy-to-load cassette which slips into the
back of the camera. Film is made up of light-sensitive
chemicals, therefore light can only be allowed to enter
the camera for the instant needed to expose the picture,
or *image*, onto the film. The mechanism which controls
the entry of light is called the shutter, whilst the image is
formed by the lens. Diagram *d* (page 6) shows how light
rays reflected from the subject are bent or *refracted* to
form a sharp picture.

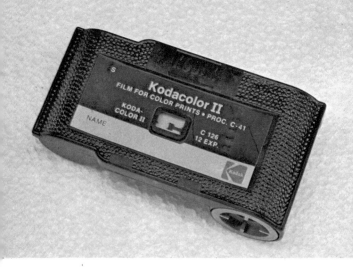

With such cameras as the Kodak Instamatic (diagram c) all one has to do is to compose the picture in the viewfinder and press the shutter. These simple cameras are capable of producing good results, and are ideal for beginners. Picture *e* is a typical example. The monkey is shown clearly and seems to express a sadness as he gazes beyond the wiring which holds him captive. With a little imagination anyone could take a picture like this.

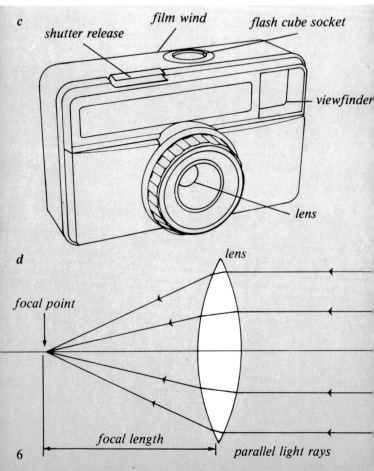

c

shutter release

film wind

flash cube socket

viewfinder

lens

d

lens

focal point

focal length

parallel light rays

Alongside we see another simple but effective picture. Notice how the camera position has given a good view of the cottage lit by the sun; notice also how the scene is enhanced by the cloud details. Equally important is the dark roof, which provides a contrast between the light sky and white cottage wall. There is also an absence of any poles or wires which would have spoilt the harmony of the scene.

One of the greatest misunderstandings about photography is a belief that the best pictures are only taken with complicated and expensive equipment. Indeed the opposite is often true – many people with the best cameras produce dreadful results simply because they have never bothered to learn about taking pictures.

Obviously these simple cameras have their limitations and are not suitable for every type of photography. In chapter 7, we shall be looking at the more advanced *reflex* camera used by many keen amateurs and even some beginners. It is important at the outset to decide which type of camera is best suited to the pictures you wish to take. Your local photographic dealer will be pleased to discuss this with you.

**Chapter 2**

# Elements in picture making

It will help us to think of pictures as containing, in various degrees, some or all of the following elements: form, light, colour and effect. What is meant by these?

**Form**   This is the shape of the objects in a picture's composition. When we begin photography, we learn how to place forms harmoniously in the viewfinders of our cameras.

**Light**   Photography cannot exist without light; the photographer models with light as a potter models with clay. Sometimes, however, photographers make a special feature of light and use concentrations of it.

**Colour**   This is usually present in all our pictures, but photographers sometimes select a subject especially for its colour. This then becomes the principal reason for the picture.

**Effect**   Some pictures are more concerned with visual effects than any other element. Often these effects are photographed to create atmosphere such as silhouettes or sunsets. Other effects might be reflections in water or shafts of sunlight pouring into a cathedral – see if you can think of others.

Obviously these elements merge into one another, but usually they occur in a recognisable order. When we look at pictures we must try to interpret their meaning. We must try to read them as we read words. Let us consider the accompanying nine scenes.

*a* *Form* is predominant here, the picture clearly reveals its subject by strong composition. *Colour* takes second place with the vigorous contrasts of red and green.

*b* It was *colour* which attracted me to these barrels rather than their *form*.

*c* An *effect* picture. The photographer was fascinated by these reflections in water. Notice how *colour* is introduced as a secondary element by the figure in red.

*d* You can imagine how the *colour* of autumn leaves provided an irresistible subject here, especially when backed by the stately *form* of the trees.

*e* An interesting study of *light* achieved by facing the camera towards the sun. This is also an *effect* picture heightened by the *form* of the clouds. *Colour* is entirely absent.

*f* *Colour* to the fore – the subject itself being of little importance. Notice the two spots of paint dripped into the foreground.

*g* An exciting *effect* created by *panning* the camera with the speeding cycle and blurring out the background to create an impression of movement. See how this technique has made the subject's *form* stand out.

*i*

*h* This scene shows *light* filtering into an old depot, transforming the derelict steam engines into a mottled *effect*. There is no *colour*, and hardly any *form*.

*i* Not a photograph but a self-portrait by the Dutch Master Rembrandt who was famous for his use of *light*. Here he reveals a miraculous combination of *light* and *form*.

*i*

11

# Chapter 3
## Composition

The composition of our pictures is of vital importance.
Apart from selecting the best angle and lighting
conditions for any given subject, we must also decide
what to put into a picture and what to leave out. This
means looking very carefully through the viewfinder and
seeing not only the subject but its relationships with the
surroundings as well.

*a* Let us begin by studying a perfect composition –
Botticelli's 'Birth of Venus', painted about 1485. The
classical harmony of this picture is outstanding: it is a
lesson to painter and photographer alike. Venus is
balanced by figures on either side, both of whom lean
towards her and guide the viewer's eye to the subject.
The foreground figures divide the picture into three
parts, and this is echoed by the fact that the horizon is
two thirds of the way up the picture.

*b* **b** The basic composition of this rural scene is not dissimilar to the previous picture. The tree is situated in the left-hand third against a sky occupying two thirds of the picture area. Such proportions provide a sense of balance.

*c* **c** Here, a different sense of proportion has been achieved by the glorious smokeball hovering in the sky and balancing the subject. If the engine's smoke had risen straight up into the air, the composition would have been spoilt by an empty space on the left.

*d* **d** Clouds play an important role in landscape photography, and in this scene of a barn they have been composed superbly. Because of its strong colour, the barn is the dominant item even though it occupies only a minute part of the picture area. If, however, the trees had been decked in autumn leaves, the emphasis would have been taken away from the barn and the picture's meaning changed entirely. When composing, remember that colours must be placed to enhance the subject – as in this picture – and not to detract from it.

*e* This study demonstrates two further aspects of composition: firstly it possesses lively foreground detail; and secondly it has two main areas of interest. Notice how these areas are clearly separated by a neutral expanse of ground in the picture's middle distance.

*f* The children's expressions radiate outwards because the background is neutral and does not intrude upon the subject.

Notice how, in each of these six scenes, the entire picture area has been filled up. Remember an old adage: "If your pictures are not good enough, you are probably not near enough."

## II – How not to do it

We are now going to look at a selection of badly-composed photographs to discover the mistakes the photographers have made.

*a*  A beautiful building ruined by clumsy photography. A poor angle, drab and colourless. The foreground kerb and three soldiers do nothing for the picture and matters are made worse by the blue bus veering crazily into the scene from the left.

*b*  Did you ever see anyone with a thistle growing out of their head? This photographer did – without even noticing it! Other mistakes include the mother's face in shadow, and a harsh horizon line cutting through her waist.

*a*

*b*

*c* A very interesting portrait. The boy and the lion have good expressions, whilst the lighting is perfect. Unfortunately the impact is lost by too much unwanted detail on either side. Instead of a horizontal composition, the camera should have been held vertically and moved closer to the subject as the guide lines indicate.

*d* What do you think the photographer was trying to achieve here? If he was only interested in the butterfly, he should have been much closer. If, however, he wanted the butterfly on a natural background, flowers of a different colour should have been used. Neither the beauty of the butterfly nor the flowers can be appreciated owing to the merging of colours.

*e* How many mistakes can you find in this one? The intention was to show a family group in the garden. But look what has happened –

too much foreground, an ugly post jutting in from the left, a dustbin on the right and washing on the line in the background! The real picture is within the rectangle drawn.

*f* A tranquil scene beautifully lit by evening sunlight, but spoilt by too much sky. A longer lens (see chapter 7) would have solved this difficulty. Note the corrected composition.

*g* There are two errors here. Firstly, the foreground occupies half of the picture; and secondly, the girls' white blouses merge into the buildings behind. Two mistakes which dissipate all impact.

*h* A fawn is a very photogenic animal, but this picture does not do it justice, for the creature is lost amongst boring surroundings. A longer lens would have brought the fawn closer without frightening it, and eliminated the sky which serves no purpose.

*i* What a dreadful mess! How many faults can you find? The photographer was so pre-occupied with the Arab and his camel that he didn't notice his own shadow in the left corner. Other errors include a hopeless confusion of the subject amongst cars and buses, a horizon which cuts the picture into two equal halves and, once again, too much foreground. I hope no one reading this book will ever take a photograph as badly as this. Can you imagine how much better the Arab and camel would have looked in the openness of a golden desert?

*j* This fine portrait is largely spoilt by the blue curtain protruding into the picture. With a little more thought the sitter could have been photographed against a neutral background.

## III – Making the Perfect Picture

Much of the skill involved in taking good photographs lies in making the best use of all possible circumstances. These pictures show what I mean.

*a* Very well composed, but the black engines are rather lost against a dark sky. There is also a lack of animation.

*b* This is better: the addition of lights and steam have added much excitement – possibly too much as the left-hand engine has disappeared completely!

*c* Perfect: the extra light and a better distribution of steam renders both engines clearly visible and enables them to stand out from the dark background.

*c*

Here are three further examples emphasising the need for patience and imagination when taking a photograph.

*d* A well-composed study of two locomotives hauling a heavy train. The scene is lit by gentle evening sunlight, and complete with interesting cloud formations. Only one item is missing – a lovely plume of smoke.

*e* Marvellous: smoke is rising from both engines, but unfortunately the sun has gone behind cloud and the fireman is leaning on the engine's buffer.

*f* Here is the perfect picture, with clear sunlight and plenty of smoke. The fireman has also moved out of view. An alternative would have been to show both engines smoking.

## IV – Colour

*a* As photographers we need to establish a keen awareness of colour. Below is a colour circle showing the gradation from the warmer colours of red, orange and yellow, through to the cooler ones of green and blue. Colours which lie opposite on the circle, i e red and green, blue and orange, and yellow and violet, are *contrasts*, whilst those which lie together are similar and *harmonise* with each other. Few pictures are composed solely of warm or cool colours, but rather as interesting combinations of the two.

*b* Now examine the Munsell colour sphere below and see how pure or *fully saturated* colours graduate towards white, black or grey. This system enables a great

*a*

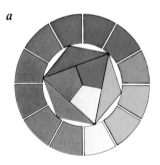

diversity of colours to be measured and is worthy of further study to help the eye to appreciate the wide range of tones within any particular colour. (For a fuller explanation, see page 36 of the Ladybird book *How it works: The Camera*).

*b*

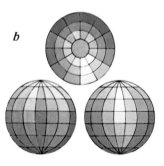

In a photograph, every colour exerts its influence upon the others present. Therefore it is absolutely vital that you compose the colours best suited to your purpose. Study the selection of colours in these pictures.

21

*c* This red engine stands out clearly from the trees by means of the contrast of red and green. A simple but meaningful colour composition.

*c*

*d*

*d* An instance of 'aerial perspective', wherein the warmer or more vigorous colour has been composed in the foreground and the weaker or *receding* ones to the rear. This creates an illusion of depth, because our eyes focus closer on the stronger colours.

*e*  An effective colour arrangement, showing how well the pink blossom shows up against the blue background.

*f*  Another foreground of pink, but this time against a paler blue background. Compare this with the previous picture and decide which of the two you prefer.

*g*

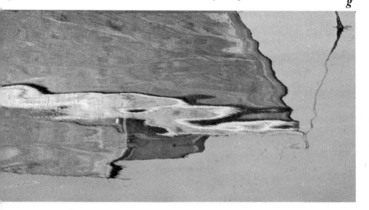

*g*  This simple evocation of a boat reflected in still water uses the contrasts of orange and blue.

*h*  A rather complicated scheme containing a wide range of colour. The result is exciting, but notice how the orange and red areas of the girl's dress draw the eye away from the two faces. This emphasises once again the need to compose colour very carefully.

*h*

# Chapter 4

## Learning to see again

In this chapter I want to show how we can study familiar scenes in their every mood, and capture them with our camera throughout the year. Nature is in a constant state of change, her moods and colours vary minute by minute, hour by hour, day by day and season by season. It is the interpretation of these infinite moods which provides photography with much of its fascination.

Despite the bustle of our everyday lives, it is vital to be permanently aware of these visual dynamics. If we only take photographs during the summer holidays, we miss most of the pleasure and creativity photography has to offer.

Compare pictures *a* and *b*. Both were taken at the same place – the first in autumn, the second during winter. Imagine the scene in summertime.

I took the next three pictures at a colliery in South Wales. The first indicates my basic composition. It is a misty winter morning and I plan to frame the engine by the broken window and so heighten the atmosphere of this grimy industrial scene. Picture *d* shows the subject in exactly the right position but notice the pieces of broken glass added to the foreground and window

*c*

frame. You can also see how snow has melted during the two hours I stood waiting for the train to pass. Fortunately the temperature remained low enough to emphasise the steam leaking from the old engine. In complete contrast comes picture *e*, made one year later on a wet cloudy day. Here, the full industrial atmosphere is brought out by the grey slag and gloomy conditions.

*d*

*e*

Pictures *f* and *g* will help you to train your eye for detail. Once again they show the same scene photographed during different seasons. The first, made in autumn, has lovely deep shadows falling across the foreground. In contrast, the sun tinges the fences with highlights and illuminates the fields to the rear.

These two areas of light and shade are separated by the four trees which in turn also include the same contrasts, ranging from the backlit leaves on the left to the shaded green areas on the right.

*f*

Notice especially how the sun has lit a few russet leaves in the lower left foreground, in addition to those on the small tree immediately behind.

Finally, the sunlit area recedes to bluish haze in the far background and creates the feeling of distance which is so important in landscape work.

Now make a careful comparison with the view alongside, *g*, taken during winter.

*g*

Apart from showing variations of light and season these studies of a village street reveal subtle changes in the actual content of the scene itself.

The first picture shows three red areas: the hedge, car and holly. All are missing from the second view.

In the third view, taken in fog and snow, even the church has disappeared. But equally dramatic is the transformation of high-lights -- such as the wall, steeple and cottages – into areas of sombre shadow.

Furthermore, two items are missing from this last picture – the telegraph post in front of the cottages and the bushes overhanging the church wall.

*j*

These exciting pictures demonstrate two further ways in which a scene can be interpreted by creative photography. One is by adjusting the composition, and the other by using different camera lenses. In the first study two engines

are residing amid the smoky gloom of their depot. But this scene is changed by the addition of a third engine and a stronger emphasis upon the light rays. Both pictures were taken with a standard (50 mm) lens. However, by using a 135 mm lens, an entirely different picture can be made from identical subject matter (illustration *m*). In order to change the lens, you need a reflex type of camera as discussed in chapter 7.

*n*

During the brief weeks of early summer when fields of yellow flowers appear, a wonderful transformation of the countryside occurs.

The photographs alongside were made over a two week period from the same camera position at an identical time of day. Illustration *n* sets the scene with afternoon sunlight falling obliquely on the church. The following view, taken a few days later, has a new dimension added by the heavier clouds. However, the 'pièce de résistance' occurred during the second week when, after a storm, a rainbow miraculously appeared. Could you imagine a more dramatic change of scene than this? Here, patience and careful observation have produced a photograph which in all probability will never occur again. The famous line, "each a glimpse and gone forever," is the photographer's guiding phrase.

Finally, a very different kind of variation in which the photographer has used his own source of light by means of flash. The first picture looked all right to the eye, but the girl's face has appeared too dark.

This is because the camera is not able to compensate for low light levels in the same way that our eyes can.

Once we have learned to anticipate these 'blind spots,' the problem can be easily solved by the use of flash – either with cubes on the Instamatic, or by a simple electronic gun on the reflex camera.

The flash can either be fired directly at the subject or reflected from a nearby white wall or piece of white card. This reflected method often gives a gentler and more even illumination.

r

# Chapter 5
## Painting with a lens

The great painters of centuries past offer much
inspiration to the colour photographer. Their ideas of
harmony and vigour have, to a large extent, set the
guidelines for successful photography. We must learn to
enjoy great paintings as a vital part of our pictorial
understanding.

In this chapter I have selected four famous works and
set them alongside photographs which resemble them
both in subject and approach. In each case the paintings
have influenced the photographs.

*a*   Below we see 'Coalbrookdale by Night', painted by
Philippe de Loutherbourg in 1801. It shows one of the
world's first iron foundries at the beginning of the
Industrial Revolution, and reveals in an unforgettable
way the fiery drama of iron making.

*a*

*b*

*b*   This painting made a deep impression upon me, and
I have tried to emulate some of its brilliance in the
picture which shows molten waste from steelmaking
being tipped down a slag bank during the early hours
of the morning.

*c*

*d*

*c, d*  Above we see another timeless work – Constable's painting of Salisbury Cathedral. This typically English landscape was painted in 1823. It shows the celebrated cathedral framed in a picturesque way by trees in what might be called a photographic manner, although it was, of course, artists like Constable that originated such techniques. The photograph, made exactly one and a half centuries later, closely follows Constable's style.

*e*  Next is the immortal 'Fighting Téméraire' painted by Turner in 1839. Apart from being a celebrated work of art, this picture is also an important historical document. It shows one of Nelson's ships from the Battle of Trafalgar being towed across the Thames on its way to be broken up. The *Téméraire* was once a noble man-o'-war and the tragedy of her demise is symbolically lit by a raging sunset. Turner actually witnessed this scene.

*e*

*f*

My photograph alongside shows an equally celebrated man-o'-war – one of Hitler's famous engines of World War II. The Germans built many thousands of these to follow their armies during their attempted conquest of Europe. This picture is also symbolically lit by a sunset as a romantic testimonial to the last of a great breed.

*g*

*h*

*g, h* Have you ever thought of taking photographs in fog? It offers many possibilities as the pictures above indicate. On the left is a copy of a painting by the French Impressionist Claude Monet showing the Houses of Parliament during one of the infamous fogs which welled up and suffocated London during Victorian times. As the sun slowly penetrates the obstinate mists, the buildings loom in silhouette and bands of golden light colour the River Thames.

Alongside is a photograph I took in the spirit of Monet's visions.

**Chapter 6**

# Finding your subject

Having acquired an interest in photography you must now decide which subjects appeal to you the most. Remember another adage: "It's not what you like to photograph, but what do you like *enough* to want to photograph?"

Most subjects demand considerable attention if you are to obtain good results. Furthermore, your choice of subject will often dictate the type of equipment you need.

Some beginners simply make pictures of whatever appeals to them; invariably the results are mediocre. Take the analogy of a sportsman: imagine someone wanting to excel in football, cricket, rugby, tennis and swimming. If he were attempting all five at once, he would not achieve very much, but by concentrating upon one – or at most two – his success and satisfaction would obviously be greater.

Once you have decided upon your favourite subject, you must acquire a pictorial understanding of it. Study its characteristics both visually and factually, and find out what type of camera and/or accessories are best suited to your purpose.

Remember that many of the greatest painters are associated with the subjects they chose. We think of Constable's pictures of the countryside – especially his native Suffolk; Lowry's industrial landscapes; Rembrandt's portraits; Turner's seascapes, or Thorburn's birds and mammals.

The accompanying pictures illustrate a few subjects which offer endless possibilities for photography.

## A   Portraiture

Few subjects are more fascinating than people. They can either be taken formally – as seen here – or caught unawares by candid photography. A great deal can be achieved using the simpler cameras – with or without flash – but for more specialised studies a reflex camera with interchangeable lenses is necessary.

*a*

## B   Architecture

History has left us with a marvellous legacy of interesting buildings. Many years of happy leisure could be spent photographing churches and castles alone, so diverse are the styles and periods. Apart from the joy of actually photographing such subjects, you have the added pleasure of discovering where the most interesting examples can be found.

*b*

*c*

## C Close Ups

These reveal a new world of colour and intrigue. Flowers, butterflies, moths, smaller insects, stamps and coins can be photographed in detail with relatively inexpensive equipment. An Instamatic camera will take some larger subjects – such as the above – but for smaller items, you need a reflex camera fitted with extension 'tubes and bellows'. These allow the lens to be moved further from the film.

## D Landscapes

This is undoubtedly the most popular subject of all, and one for which any camera is suitable. Remember the words of the great painter Constable: "clouds are the keynote to landscapes" – a truth well borne out by this picture.

*d*

## E Transport

Photographers have always been attracted to the various forms of transport. Photography 'freezes time' and the transport wonders of today may be history in a few years to come.

Railways, aircraft and buses are three obvious choices but perhaps you may prefer the picturesque industrial history of the canal network. This comprehensive scene includes two barges, the towpath and a lock-keeper's cottage.

*e*

## F Natural history

Natural history photography has increased in popularity over recent years, largely through the availability of longer focal-length lenses. There has also been an increase in the number of Nature Reserves open to the public. A rather specialised subject but one which is challenging and deeply rewarding.

*f*

**Chapter 7**

# The 35mm reflex camera

As your photography progresses you are likely to need a single lens reflex. Here are five advantages offered by this type of camera compared with the simpler models:

1   The ability to interchange lenses;

2   A complete range of settings on the camera and lens to deal with almost every situation;

3   Focussing of the lens through the viewfinder;

4   Improved picture sharpness through better lenses and larger film size;

5   The ability to use other accessories such as bellows and tubes for close ups.

*a*

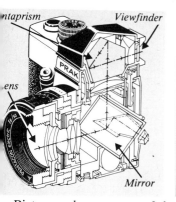

Pentaprism   Viewfinder

PRAK

Lens

PENTACON electric   f8 60

Mirror

AGFACOLOR CT18
AGFACOLOR CT21
AGFACHROME pocket special
AGFACOLOR CT 126

c

Picture *a* shows a part of the comprehensive Praktica system. The Praktica is greatly recommended as, apart from its quality, it is inexpensive compared with many similar cameras. The illustration shows two Praktica bodies, one with the lens removed and the other with an open back showing the film in position. Lenses of varying focal lengths can also be seen; these screw on to the camera as required. In the centre is the famous Weston meter for measuring the strength of the light – although many Praktica models have a light meter built in.

Illustration *b* indicates how the viewing system of the reflex camera works. The mirror reflects the image through the Pentaprism and into the viewfinder. Thus viewing and focussing actually take place through the lens.

Having illustrated the 'reflex', we must now consider the two main advantages of interchangeable lenses. Firstly we can vary the angle of view, and secondly vary the perspective. Illustrations *d – j* show what is meant by 'angle of view'. For these studies, the camera was placed in a set position pointing towards the distant tower.

20 mm

29 mm

50 mm

80 mm

135 mm

200 mm

300 mm

The first shot, made with a 20 mm wide angle lens, shows the tower in the far distance but as longer lenses were applied, up to 300 mm, the subject becomes increasingly dominant. There are many occasions when lenses of varying angles of view are required. The wide angle is useful for working in restricted

*k*

areas – such as a small room – whereas longer lenses are necessary for photographing distant objects.

How to change perspective is dramatically shown by pictures *k* and *l*. Look carefully at the size relationships between the tree stump and barn. Picture *k* was taken with a 29 mm wide angle lens only a few feet away from the stump. See how the stump looms to enormous proportions as the barn reduces to matchbox size.

However, by moving further back along the same camera axis and fitting a 200 mm lens, the barn returns to a more 'realistic' proportion. Obviously this change of perspective can only be achieved by altering the camera's position as well as the lens. If different lenses were used without moving the camera, only the angle of view would be affected – as in pictures *d – j*.

*l*

Now let us consider how to use variations in perspective as part of our creative photography. Examine pictures *m* and *n* closely – both show the same locomotive being broken up for scrap. The first theme shows the men preparing to cut into the boiler with their acetylene torches. The foreground is dominated by aspects of our subject's anatomy – such elements as pistons, wheel fragments and a chimney. This view was made in low angle morning sunlight, using a Praktica camera and 50 mm standard lens.

In the succeeding picture the flare of acetylene torches is heightened by the twilight and echoed by the setting sun. The engine's boiler has been half cut away revealing tubes coloured a ghastly white by scale. See how the foreground fragments – lit by flash – loom up in almost nightmare fashion, so heightened is the perspective. This picture was taken with a wide angle lens.

These two studies contain several important differences apart from variations in perspective. The condition of the subject varies enormously as does the illumination – sunlight in *m* and a combination of sunset and fill-in flash on *n*.

*n*

Another exciting possibility offered by the reflex camera is called *differential focussing* which means to vary the zones of sharpness. Picture *o* illustrates this technique. Notice how the relationship between the engine and berries has been emphasised. By the same method, backgrounds

*o*

can be blurred either to obliterate distracting detail or merely to add impact to the subject. These techniques – easily mastered with suitable lenses – are a fundamental part of photographic expression.

The various aspects we have discussed so far provide a basis for much personal interpretation in picture making, which is my theme for the following chapter.

## Chapter 8
# A personal style

If you and a friend each took a photograph of the same
subject, the pictures produced would be different.
Everyone has his own approach, and in learning to take
photographs we form a distinct personal style.
Remember that the work of a good photographer is
every bit as individualistic as that of a good painter. The
way in which you state your individuality through a
camera depends on many things: your choice of subject,
lighting, composition, colour, lens, and last but not
least, what your photographs express.

To show just what is meant by personal style, in this
chapter we join with the painter once again to discuss six
very different scenes with buildings as a common theme.
These works represent personal styles through which
each painter has conveyed his feelings with great clarity.
The first painting is by Antonio Canaletto, an 18th
century Venetian artist. Many of Canaletto's paintings
tend to resemble photographs: the sun invariably falls
from behind and he reveals an almost mechanical
precision of detail.

*a*

*b*

Alongside is a painting by Francesco Guardi who worked at the same period as Canaletto and in a similar style. Here the rougher handling of paint shows a rather more earthy approach to the subject, illuminated by sunlight of remarkable purity.

In complete contrast, picture *c* is an opaque water colour, 'Norham Castle, Sunrise' by the English painter JMW Turner. Here, form is almost completely dissolved in a misty vapour. A touch of magic is provided by the cow standing in the foreground shallows. This is one of Turner's later paintings when he was trying, above all, to represent light and colour, and the effect has almost a dreamlike, poetic quality.

*c*

Picture *d* is a work by the French Impressionist Camille
Pissarro. The Impressionists were an exciting group of
painters who worked largely in the open air. They saw
nature not as a mass of solid objects but rather as a
dazzling medley of radiant colours which were in a
constant state of change with the varying effects of light
on them. Before the Impressionists, no one had looked
at nature in this way and their pictures were to have a
tremendous influence upon the work of later artists.

One painter who was influenced by the Impressionists
was Paul Cézanne. His ambition was to combine
Impressionism's representation of coloured light with
more solid form. His success is shown by this view of
Mount St Victoire (*e*) – a theme he painted in diverse
moods over many years. Compare the supple weight of
Cézanne's foreground pine with the tree in Pissarro's
picture. Notice also the solidity of the buildings and
stone viaduct, in addition to the hard unyielding rock of
the mountain.

*e*

Finally, an industrial landscape by L S Lowry. This artist was one of the few to concentrate on the industrial scene. Many of his paintings convey the very essence of the Industrial Revolution, with teeming populations centred on stark factories. If you look at other pictures by Lowry, you will find he never painted shadows, nor did he include motor cars. So what is left out of a picture – or a photograph – is as much a part of a personal style as those things which appear.

*f*

## Chapter 9

# Where do we go from here?

## GOOD COMPANIONSHIP

Now you have become keen on photography, it is important that your interest be maintained. Your enthusiasm and creative potential can be developed by mixing with fellow photographers. One obvious way of doing this is to join a local camera club – your library will provide the details. These clubs usually meet weekly and offer a varied programme of lectures, demonstrations, practical work and competitions.

## A PHOTOGRAPHIC MAGAZINE

Place a regular order with your newsagent for a good photographic magazine. The most successful of the monthlies is *Practical Photography* which, apart from including regular articles for beginners, has excellent general features plus advice columns and details of the latest in equipment. This magazine will also tell you about photographic exhibitions around the country.

## EXCITING BOOKS

A small library of carefully selected books will also provide you with a constant source of reference and inspiration. There is an excellent choice of books upon photography and apart from the companion book – Ladybird *How it works, The Camera* – I would recommend *Photography* by Eric De Maré, published in paperback by Penguin. You may also like to collect a few books about your favourite painters; for instance, no one keen upon landscape photography should be without the Phaidon Press book of Constable's paintings. (You can also borrow books from your library.)

*The picture above was taken in a scrapyard using a reflex camera. By using differential focussing I was able to heighten the contrast between the foreground grasses and the lamp, which is shown slightly out of focus. Note the careful selection of colours and also the way in which the lamp has been composed at an angle to emphasise its shape. Compare this method of using differential focus with picture o on page 43.*

## VISITS TO EXHIBITIONS AND GALLERIES

Attend a few photographic exhibitions. It is valuable to see what other photographers are doing, even if their subject matter and style does not particularly appeal to you. Visits to art galleries are equally pertinent, especially famous ones like the National or Tate Gallery in London. Here you will find a diversity of paintings from artists over several centuries.

Try to select particular works or styles from which you can draw inspiration. Don't make the mistake of trying to see too much at once; look at a few pictures at a time and enjoy them. Great paintings demand your attention, and art galleries – like all exhibitions – become tiring if you try to do too much.

## A FINAL WORD

Take your pictures under the best possible circumstances: watch and wait for the right conditions. Photography requires time and patience. Many of the paintings and photographs in this book were the result of much thought and planning – this is all part of the satisfaction to be gained from creating worthwhile pictures. On the right we see an express train at speed; this photograph took several days to make.

Do your photography as close to home as possible; almost every landscape we have seen in the preceding chapters was taken within three miles (5 kilometres) of home. When you finally confront a potential masterpiece, try to take more than one picture, using slightly different camera settings in order to obtain the optimum (best) exposure; this is especially important when making colour transparencies.

Always carry a notebook to record what photographs you have taken; write down the date and place, conditions and camera settings, plus what you were trying to achieve. Use these notes to check the results and if any pictures are unsatisfactory, find out exactly where you went wrong and re-shoot them whenever possible.

Edit your slides on a light box; select only the best, catalogue them and store in a dark dry place. Eventually you will have sufficient to give interesting slide shows.

No limit exists to the pleasure that fine pictures can give – especially when you have been their creator. There are few better companions in life than a camera.

# Index

|  | page |
|---|---|
| Aerial perspective | 22 |
| Angle of view | 39, 40 |
| Art galleries | 50 |
| Bad photography see Picture composition | |
| Bellows | 38 |
| 'Birth of Venus' | 12 |
| Books on photography | 48 |
| Botticelli | 12 |
| Camera clubs | 48 |
| Cameras | 4-7, 28, 30, 35, 36, 38-39, 42, 43 |
| Canaletto, Antonio | 44 |
| Cézanne, Paul | 46-47 |
| Close ups | 14, 16, 17, 36 |
| Clubs | 48 |
| 'Coalbrookdale by Night' | 31 |
| Colour | 8, 9, 11, 21 |
| In composition | 10, 13, 15, 16, 17, 22-23 |
| Composition see Picture composition | |
| Constable, John | 32, 34, 36, 48 |
| Differential focussing | 43 |
| Effect of composition | 8, 9, 10, 11 |
| Exhibitions | 50 |
| 'Fighting Téméraire' | 32 |
| Film | 4, 5, 38, 39 |
| Flash photography | 30, 35, 42-43 |
| Form: in composition | 8, 9, 10, 11 |
| Guardi, Francesco | 45 |

|  | pag |
|---|---|
| 'Houses of Parliament' | 3 |
| Image | 4, 3 |
| Impressionist paintings | 33, 4 |
| Kodak Instamatic camera | 5, 6 30, 3 |
| Lenses | 4, 6, 28, 35, 36, 37, 38 39, 40-41, 42, 4 |
| Light | 4, 6, 8, 10, 11, 12, 19 26, 27, 29, 30, 42, 4 |
| Light box | 5 |
| Light meter | 38, 3 |
| Loutherbourg, Philippe de | 3 |
| Lowry, L S | 34, 4 |
| Magazines: photographic | 4 |
| Monet, Claude | 3 |
| 'Mount St Victoire' | 46-4 |
| Munsell colour sphere | 2 |
| 'Norham Castle, Sunrise' | 4 |
| Paintings: Comparison with photography | 11-13, 31-33 44-47, 48, 5 |
| Panning | 1 |
| Perspective | 15, 22, 39, 40-4 |
| Picture composition | 6-20 22-33, 35-37, 41-4 |
| perspective | 40-4 |
| style | 44-4 |
| wrong composition | 15-2 |
| Photography: meaning | |
| Pissarro, Camille | 4 |
| Practical Photography | 4 |
| Praktica camera | 38-39, 4 |